COMPLIMENTS OF
THE TRUSTEES OF THE

TO: ______________________

NAPOLEON HILL
FOUNDATION

From: ______________________

感谢拿破仑希尔基金会的全权委托

著作权登记号：图字：01-2013-3423号

图书在版编目（CIP）数据
拿破仑希尔成功学17法则 / (美) 希尔 (Hill,N.) 著；程慧，李爱群译.
-- 北京：经济日报出版社，2013.7
ISBN 978-7-80257-529-5

Ⅰ.①拿… Ⅱ.①希… ②程… ③李… Ⅲ.①成功心理－通俗读物 Ⅳ.①B848.4-49

中国版本图书馆CIP数据核字(2013)第142890号

拿破仑·希尔成功学17法则

著　　者	拿破仑·希尔
译　　者	程　慧　李爱群
责任编辑	胡子清
责任校对	丁　姝
出版发行	经济日报出版社
社　　址	北京西城区右安门内大街65号
邮政编码	100054
电　　话	编辑部 63584556 发行部63538621
网　　址	www.edpbook.com.cn
E-mail	jjrb58@sina.com
经　　销	全国新华书店
印　　刷	中国电影出版社印刷厂
开　　本	889*1194mm 32开
图 文 数	144面
印　　张	4
版　　次	2013年7月第一版
印　　次	2013年7月第一次印刷
书　　号	ISBN 978-7-80257-529-5
定　　价	28.00 元

拿破仑·希尔

成功学17法则

Lessons on Success

17 Principles of Personal Achievement

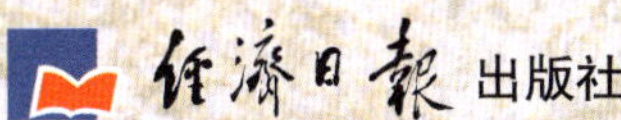

CONTENTS

目录

Foreword

In my position as executive director of the Napoleon Hill Foundation, I have often been asked, "Why should a person need more than one good book on success!" The answer to that question can be shown by recalling our early learning. We were taught our ABCs by repeating them through games, stories, or simply reciting them until they became a part of our memory, For example. each ot US probably learned our multiplication tables in the same manner. Each set of numbers was repeated so many times that if asked what 8x8 equaled, the answer 64 would be recalled with very little effort.

Another excellent reason to continue exposure to inspirational material, whether it be a self-help magazine, book, audio, video, or attending a seminar, is to be among the estimated 5 percent who are truly successful. You will likely discover that your desires will change markedly as you advance in years.

As a young person, it is normal to be concerned with accomplishments to provide housing, education, and everyday

序

我在担任拿破仑·希尔基金会的执行董事期间，经常被问到这样一个问题，“为什么一个人需要不止一本关于成功方面的好书？”要回答这个问题，我们可以回顾一下我们早期的学习经历。我们学习入门知识都是通过游戏、故事等反复重复，或者不停地背诵直至这些知识成为记忆的一部分。比如说，我们每个人大概都是通过相同的方式来学习乘法表的。每一组数字我们都重复了无数次，所以当被问到8乘以8等于多少时，我们几乎不费吹灰之力就可以说出答案是64。

还有一个理由能让你继续接触这些给予灵感的材料，无论是教你励志的杂志、书籍、录音、录像还是参加某些研讨班，都是要帮你成为5%的真正的成功人士中的一员。你很可能会发现随着年龄的增长，你的期望也在发生显著变化。

作为一个年轻人，我们关心那些能够满足诸如住房、教育等日常需求的事情，这是很正常的。我们首先把大多数精力都花在获取基本安全感上面。尽管我们也会捐款给教堂或是慈善机构，但那并不是我们优先考虑的对象。

成功学的基本原则从来都不会改变，而显然我们对成功的渴望一直在变化。总有一天我们会投入更多的精力去帮助世界上那些不幸的人们，这是一定的。

needs and wants. Most of our efforts are directed at obtaining security. Though We will no doubt contribute to our church or favorite charities,they will not be our primary focus.

While the principles of success philosophy do not change, it will become evident that our desires to make a difference do. It will become normal to put more energy to helping those in the world who are less fortunate.

Napoleon Hill knew the keys to success and shared that wisdom with millions. As you read the following pages, you'll discover the principles you need to follow to be among the truly successful and discover ways that application in your life will help you reach your goals.

In the final analysis, all successful people will be remembered more for what they gave rather than what they got in life.

Don M. Green, Executive Director, Napoleon Hill Foundation

Don M Green

拿破仑·希尔掌握成功的关键，并将他的智慧与成千上万的人们分享。当你在阅读本书时，你会了解你必须遵循哪些原则来成为真正成功的人，会发现在生活中你可以运用哪些方法来达到目标。

总而言之，所有成功人士都会因为他们的付出而不是他们的所得而为世人所牢记。

唐·M.·格林 拿破仑·希尔基金会执行董事

Don M Green

INTRODUCTION

Exactly 100 years ago, a fortuitous meeting in Pittsburgh completely changed the life of one young man and ushered in a new philosophy of personal achievement that has served as the foundation of the success movement for the last century.

That young man was Napoleon Hill, a young reporter from Virginia.That meeting in the fall of 1908 was,as he described it, when"the Hand of Destiny reached out."

Hill had been granted an interview with Andrew Carnegie, the steel magnate who was then the world's richest man. Hill dove into the questioning: "Mr.Carnegie, to what do you attribute your phenomenal success?"

The industrialist, then 73, opened up quickly and, with wit and his unrivaled gift for anecdote, began to relate the stories of his achievements.Hill could hardly keep up his shorthand notes when Carnegie then began to expound on his and others'theories of personal achievement.

Carnegie lamented, "It's a shame that each new generation must find the way to success by trial and error when the

引言

整整一百年前，发生在匹兹堡的一次偶然会面彻底改变了一个年轻人的一生，他创建了新的成功学法则，从而为上一世纪成功学的发展奠定了基础。这位年轻人就是拿破仑·希尔，来自弗吉尼亚的一名年轻记者。正如他自己所描述的那样，1908年秋天的这次会面，是“幸运女神伸出了双手”。

希尔获准采访安德鲁·卡耐基，钢铁巨头，当时世界上最富有的人。希尔直奔主题，“卡耐基先生，请问是什么使您获得了如此巨大的成功？”

这位时年73岁的工业家立刻畅谈起来，带着他特有的风趣和无与伦比的讲故事天赋，开始讲述起他个人成功的故事。当卡耐基滔滔不绝详细地讲述他自己以及别人的成功之道时，希尔几乎来不及记笔记。

卡耐基悲叹道，“每一代人都必须通过不断试验和犯错误来寻找成功的方法，而这些方法的基本原则其实是十分简洁明确的，这实在是一件令人遗憾的事情。”

采访结束三天之后，卡耐基再次邀请希尔，并提供给他一次机会，由他来整理世界上第一部个人成功实践学。“我会介绍你认识一些人，他们能够并且愿意与你一起参与整理工作。你想得到这次机会吗？如果给你这次机会，你能够坚持完成吗？”

principles really are clear-cut."

Three days after the interview, Carnegie invited Hill back and offered him the opportunity to organize the world's first practical philosophy of individual achievement."I will introduce you to men who can and will collaborate with you in its organization. Do you want the opportunity, and will you follow through if it is given to you?"

Hill blurted out with characteristic enthusiasm, "Yes! I'll undertake the job-and I'll finish it."

Carnegie withdrew a stopwatch and told Hill it had taken him exactly 29 seconds to respond. Carnegie told him."The offer would have been withdrawn after 60 seconds.

It has been my esperience that a man who cannot reach a decision promptly cannot be depended on to carry through any decision he may make.I have also discovered that men who reach decisions promptly usually have the capacity to move with definiteness of purpose in other circumstances.

"very well, "said Carnegie." You have one of the two important qualities that will be needed by the man who organizes the philosophy I have described.Now I will learn whether or not you have the second.If I give you this opportunity, are you willing to devote 20 years of your time to research the causes of success and failure without pay, earning your own living as you go along?"

Hill was stunned.He had assumed that Carnegie would subsidize him from his enormous fortune.

"It is not unwillingness to supply the money," Carnegie

希尔以其特有的热情不假思索地脱口而出："当然！我愿意承担这份工作——而且我一定会坚持完成好。"

卡耐基按下秒表，告诉希尔他一共花了29秒钟来回复这个问题。卡耐基告诉他，"如果超过60秒钟才回复这个问题，那么我就会收回这次机会。因为按照我的经验，一个人如果不能快速做出某个决定，那么他就不值得信赖，他可能无法完成他做出的任何决定。我还发现能够快速做出决定的人往往有能力在其他情况下也同样带着明确的目标前进。"

"很好，"卡耐基又说道，"要整理我叙述的成功学的人必须具备两大重要品质，你已经拥有了第一个，现在让我看看你是否具备第二个重要品质。假设我给你这次机会，你是否愿意在没有报酬、靠自力更生维持生计的情况下花20年的时间致力于研究成功和失败的原因呢？"

希尔大吃一惊，他原本以为卡耐基会从他巨大的财富中出钱资助他。

"我并非不愿意出这笔钱，"卡耐基解释道，"我只是想了解你是否真正不在意多付出一些——也就是，是否在获取回报之前先提供更多服务。"

拿破仑·希尔通过了卡耐基的第二次测试。他要坚持编纂美国成功学。在接下来的20年里，他会采访托马斯·爱迪生、亨利·福特、亚历山大·格拉汉姆·贝尔、金克·吉列、西奥多·罗斯福等人。1928年，他出版了《成功法则》，收集了当时可以找到的最伟大的成功者的成功秘籍，在世界历史上第一次展示了个人成功所依据的原则。

九年后，受益于这些学说，他出版了《思考致富》一书，该书被认为是有史以来最伟大的成功学书籍。书中讲述了如何改善一个人的健康、财富及成功的重要原则。今天的读者在阅读本书

explained." It is my desire to know if you have in you the natural capacity to go the extra mile—that is, to render service before trying to collect for it."

Napoleon Hill met Carnegie's second test.He would go on to write the American philosophy of personal achievement.

For the next 20 years,he would interview such men as Thomas Edison, Henry Ford, Alexander Graham Bell, King Gillette, Theodore Roosevelt, John Rockefeller, and others. In 1928, he would publish Law of Success, a compilation of success secrets from the greatest achievers of the time that, for the first time in the history of the world, would reveal the true philosophy upon which all personal success is built.

From those teachings would come, nine years later, Think and Grow Rich! considered by many to be the greatest success book of all time. It offered essential principles for improving one's health, wealth, and success. While readers today will note that the language of the book reveals mid-20th century America, the principles expounded on for a successful life remain as powerful and pertinent today as they did 70 years ago.

This gift book offers Napoleon Hill's 17 principles of personal achievement in an easy-to-read format so you can easily learn them and start applying them to your life today. Remember: If you conceive it and believe it, you can achieve it!

时会注意到书中的语言展示的是20世纪中期的美国，但书中详述的关于成功人生的原则在今天仍然和70年前一样强大有效、恰当中肯。

本书以一种轻松易读的编排格式讲述了拿破仑·希尔的17条成功法则，以便你轻松地学习并在生活中将之付诸实践。

请记住：只要是你心之所想、信心所在，你就能够无事不成！

拿破仑·希尔
NAPOLEON HILL

1883~1970

只要是你心之所想、信心所在，
你就能够无事不成。

"Whatever the mind can conceive and believe，the mind can achieve."

成功学17法则

17 Principles of Personal Achievement

Lesson 1
Definiteness of Purpose

Don't be Like a Ship Without a Rudder,
Powerless and Directionless.

第1课
要有明确的目标

不要像一艘失去舵的小船一样，
既无能力，又无方向

Definiteness of purpose is the starting point of all achievement. All individual achievement begins with the adoption of a definite major purpose and a specific plan for its attainment. Without a purpose and a plan, people drift aimlessly through life.

Ideas form the foundation of all fortunes and the starting point of all inventions. Once you learn how to harness the power of your mind and then how to organize the knowledge, you begin to keep your mind on the things you want and off the things you do not want.

明确的目标是所有成功的起点。任何个人成功都始于有明确的目标以及为达到这个目标而设定的具体计划。没有目标，没有计划，人的一生只能是漫无目的地随波逐流。

想法是一切财富的基础，也是一切创造的起点。一旦你学会如何利用思维的力量，如何合理组织构架、利用知识，你就等于把全部注意力放在了你的目标上，同时你不想要的一切不再占用你的时间。

确立清晰的目标

◎ 你要有一个崇高的、渴望的、杰出的目标，并且时时刻刻将这一目标摆在眼前。

◎ 明确并牢记你渴望的目标。

◎ 评估并想清楚你愿意为了这个目标付出多少。

◎ 设定一个确定的日期作为自己达到目标的时间。

◎ 细细规划如何成功。简明准确地写出你的目标，达到目标的时间，以及你的付出要收获些什么。

◎ 日复一日，早上和晚间，铭记并大声朗读你写下的内容。

Develop a Definiteness of Purpose

◎ You should have one high, desirable, outstanding goal and keep it ever before you.

◎ Determine and fix in your mind exactly what you desire.

◎ Evaluate and determine exactly what you will give in return.

◎ Set a definite date for exactly when you intend to possess your desire.

◎ Clearly define your plan for achievement. Write out precisely and concisely exactly what you want, exactly when you want to achieve it, and exactly what you intend to give in return.

◎ Each and every day, morning and evening, read your written statement aloud.

要让人生之舟驶达目的地，
需先使其启航。
明确你想从生活中获取什么，
更需清楚你将付出什么。
你能收获而且也只会收获
你所渴求并为之努力的一切。

Your ship will not come in unless
you have first sent one out.

Be sure about what you want
from life and doubly sure of what
you have to give in return.

You will get exactly and only
what you ask and work for.

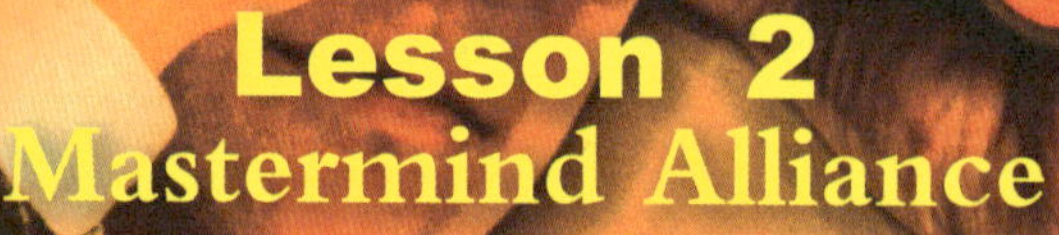

Lesson 2

Mastermind Alliance

No Man Can Become Permanent Success
Without Taking Others Along With Him.

第 2 课
决策者同盟

如果没有其他人的协助，
任何人都不可能获得永久的成功。

The Mastermind principle consists of an alliance of two or more minds working in perfect harmony for the attainment of a common definite objective. Success does not come without the cooperation of others.

An active alliance of two or more minds, in a spirit of perfect harmony, stimulates each mind to a higher degree of courage than that ordinarily experienced, and paves the way for the state of mind known as Faith.

决策者原则包含一个由两人或两人以上组成的同盟，大家和谐共事，以期达到共同的明确的目标。没有他人的合作就无法取得成功。

两人或多人组成的具有高度和谐互补的积极同盟会彼此激励，从而使双方有更多胆识，并为达到理想的信念和积极的思维状态奠定基础。

创建决策者同盟

◎ 决策者同盟的创建有多种方式，可以是你身边的人，也可以是那些愿意全心全意帮助你达成目标，愿意向你提出建议、忠告、帮助你的人。

◎ 你可以和你的配偶、朋友或者同事创建一个决策者同盟。一旦决策者同盟形成，这个团队必须立刻开始并保持积极的工作状态。团队必须在既定的时间朝着明确的目标着手制定行之有效的工作计划。

ESTABLISH A MASTERMIND ALLIANCE

◎ Your mastermind alliance can be created by surrounding yurself or aligning yourself with the advice, counsel, and personal cooperation of several people who are willing to lend you their wholehearted aid for the attainment of your objective.

◎ You can create a mastermind alliance with your spouse, friend, or co-worker. Once a mastermind alliance is formed, the group must become and remain active. The group must move in a definite plan, at a definite time, toward a definite common objective.

要创建成功的决策者同盟，
第一步就是要达到身心和谐。

The first step toward a successful mastermind alliance is to get on good terms with yourself.

Lesson 3
Applied Faith
Faith is an Active State of Mind

第 3 课
将信念付诸实践

信念是一种积极的思维状态。

Faith is a state of mind through which your aims, desires, plans, and purposes may be translated into their physical or financial equivalent.

Applied faith means action-specifically, the habit of applying your faith under any and all circumstances. It is faith in your God, yourself, your fellow being-and the unlimited opportunities available to you.

Faith without *action* is dead.

Faith is the art of believing by *doing*.

信念是一种自己心中认定的看法。通过信念，你可以将目标、期望、计划和目的转换为等量的物质或是资金。

将信念付诸实践意味着行动——说得明确些，也就是养成在所有情况下都将自己的信念付诸实践的习惯。对上帝、对自己、对同伴充满信心，一定有无穷的机会在等待着你。

缺乏行动的信念是毫无用处的。

信念就是通过行动实现信仰的艺术。

行动起来实现信念

◎ 要实现信念就要付诸行动，也是对目标或目的的一种坚信，用一系列的行动来接近目的。如果想要达到目的，可以试试祈祷。当你默念的时候，你就表达了自己对所获得的一切的感激之情。

◎ 每天早晚通过默祷确认你期望的目标。激发你的想象力，想象你已经达成了自己的目标。

◎ 默祷具有强大的力量！

USE APPLIED FAITH

◎ Applied faith is belief in an objective or purpose backed by unqualified activity. If you want results, try a prayer. When you pray, you express your gratitude and thanksgiving for the blessing you already have received.

◎ Affirm the objectives of your desires through prayer each night and morning. Inspire your imagination to see yourself already in possession of them.

◎ Prayer is your greatest power!

信念可以突破禁锢。

在你身后关上畏惧之门，

你会立刻看到信念之门在你面前开启。

如果你都没有足够的自信，

不可能要求别人相信。

Faith removes limitations.

Close the door to fear behind you
and see how quickly the door to
faith will open in front of you.

If you don't believe it yourself,
don't ask anyone else to do so.

LESSON 4
Going The Extra Mile
Put Your Mind to Work.
Access Your Ability and Energy.

第 4 课
多一些付出

专心致志地投入工作，
积蓄你的能力与精力。

Doing the extra mile is the action of rendering more and better service than that for which you are presently paid. When you go the extra mile, the Law of Compensation comes into play. This universal law neither permits any living thing to get something for nothing nor allows any form of labor to go unrewarded.

You will find that Mother Nature goes the extra mile in everything that she does. She does not create just barely enough of each gene or species to get by; she produces an overabundance to take care of all emergencies that arise and still have enough left to guarantee the perpetuation of each form of life.

相对于你期望的所得，你不要计较多一些付出，做出更多更优质的努力。多多付出，补偿法则就开始发挥效应了。这一放之四海而皆准的法则既不允许任何人不劳而获，也不会让任何人劳而无获。

你会发现我们的自然母亲在所有事情上都从不吝啬多付出一些。她创造的每一种基因或者物种都不会仅仅是勉强够数，而是会创造出足够多的数量来应对会发生的各种危机状况，并且在紧急情况发生之后仍然能留下足够的数量来维持每种生命形式的存续。

多一些付出

◎ 付出相比你所得回报更多更好的努力，并且带着积极的心态去完成这一切。养成多付出一些的习惯，因为它会带给你乐趣，会影响你和你的内心。

◎ 毫无疑问，你播下的每一颗有效工作的种子都会成倍地增长，然后给予你更为丰厚的回报。

DO THE EXTRA MILE

◎ Render more and better service for which you are paid, and do it with a positive mental attitude. Form the habit of going the extra mile because of the pleasure you get out of it and because of what it does to your and for you deep down inside.

◎ It is inevitable that every seed of useful service you sow will multiply itself and come back to you in overwhelming abundance.

不要吝惜多一些付出，机会一定会随之而来。

Start going the extra mile and opportunity will follow you.

Lesson 5
Pleasing Personality

The Attitudes You Transmit to Others Will Tell More About Yourself Than the Words You Say or How You Look.

第5课
迷人的个性

你的态度传递的信号，
会比你的言语或你的外表更能表现你的意愿。

Your personality is your greatest asset or your greatest liability, for it embraces everything that you control: mind, body, and soul. A person' s personality is the person. It shapes the nature of your thoughts, your deeds, your relationships with others, and it establishes the boudaries of the space you occupy in the world.

Personality is the sum total of one' s mental, spiritual, and physical traits and habits that distinguish one from all others. It is the factor that determines whether one is liked or disliked by others.

个性是你最大的财富，也是你最大的责任，因为它包含了你能控制的一切：思维、身体和灵魂。个性也就是人本身的特性。它决定了你的思维状态、你的行为以及你与他人的关系，它决定了你在这个世界上所从事工作的范围。

个性就是一个人区别于他人的心理的、精神的、生理的特点与习惯的总和。它是决定一个人是否受别人欢迎的重要因素。

培养迷人的个性

◎要让自己对人、对事、对环境的变化反应敏捷，也要让其他个人或团体对你所说、所想及所为所做出的反应加以关注，逐渐养成这样的习惯，这一点非常重要。

◎迷人个性的积极因素包括宽容大度、基本的礼貌、思维敏捷、言行得体、个人魅力、公正无私、诚恳真挚、有幽默感、有耐心。

ASSEMBLE AN ATTRACTIVE PERSONALITY

◎ It is imperative that you develop the habit of being sensitive to your own reactions to individuals, circumstances, and events and to the reactions of individuals and groups to what you say, think, or do.

◎ Positive factors of a pleasing personality include tolerance, common courtesy, alertness, tactfulness, personal magnetism, sportsmanship, sincerity, sense of humor, and patience.

你相信自己会成为什么样的人，
你就可以成为什么样的人。

心态是至关重要的，它决定你的个性。
迷人的笑脸往往可以击败最残酷的对手。

What you believe yourself to be, you are.

Your mental attitude is the most dependable key to your personality.

A smiling face often defeats the cruelest of antagonists.

Lesson 6
Personal Initiative
Personal Initiative is the Dynamo That Spurs
the Faculty of Your Imagination Into Action

第 6 课
个人能动性

个人能动性就像一台发动机，
它产生推动力，
进而使你的想象得以付诸于行动。

"There are two types of men," said Andrew Carnegie, "who never amount to anything. One is the fellow who never does anything except that which he is told to do; the other is the fellow who never does more than he is told to do. The man who gets ahead does the thing that should be done without being told to do it."

Personal initiative is the inner power that starts all action. It is the Power that inspires the completion of that which one begins.

It is, in fact, *self-motivation.* Motivation is that which induces *action* or determines choice.

"这世界上有两种人，最终将一事无成。"安德鲁·卡耐基曾经说过，"一种人整天无所事事什么也不干，除非有人吩咐他。还有一种人除了别人分配给他的任务之外，不肯多做一点事。而那些出人头地的人从来不需要别人的吩咐就会完成所有他认定该做的事情。"

个人能动性是引发所有行动的内在力量，正是这种力量激励着你去完成自己开创的事业。

事实上，这就是自我激励。激励可以促使你开始行动或者做出选择。

激发个人能动性

◎ 动机是存在于个人心中、促使行动的一种内在欲望，比如说一个想法，一种情感，一个愿望或是一种冲动。动机来源于想要创造某种特定结果的愿望或是力量。

◎ 以积极的心态来激发自己。愿望是形成激励的神奇力量，但成功的秘诀却在于开始行动。

◎ 快培养和运用自己的主动精神吧！

CREATE PERSONAL INITIATIVE

◎ A motive is that inner urge only within the individual which incites you to *action*, such as an idea, an emotion, a desire, or an impulse. It is a hope or other force which starts in an attempt to produce specific results.

◎ Motivate yourself with a positive mental attitude. Hope is the magic ingredient in motivation, but the secret of accomplishment is getting into *action*.

◎ Use and develop the self-starter!

成功人士积极主动地采取行动，
他们在出发前已经确立了清晰的目标。
Successful people move on their own
initiative, and they know where they are
going before they start.

Lesson 7
Positive Mental Attitude

A Positive Mental Attitude is the Greatest of Life's Riches.

第 7 课
保持积极的心态

积极的心态是人生最大的财富。

A positive mental attitude is the right, honest, constructive thought, action, or reaction to any person, situation, or set of circumstances.

It allows you to build on hope and overcome the negative attitudes of despair and discouragement. It gives you the mental power, the feeling, the confidence to do anything you make your mind up to do. It is the "I can...I will" attitude applicable to all circumstances in your life.

A positive mental attitude is the catalyst necessary for achieving worthwhile success.

所谓积极的心态是指对人、形势或是其他事物所做出的正确的、坦诚的、建设性的思考、行动或反应。

积极的心态可以让你拥有希望，克服绝望和沮丧。它给予你精神的力量、情感以及信心去完成任何你决心要做的事情。“我能…我愿意”的态度适用于一个人人生中所能碰到的一切情况。

积极的心态是获取成功所必需的催化剂。

培养积极的心态

◎ 基于自身的动机，通过意志力创造并保持积极的心态。

◎ 控制好自己的情绪，对外界的人和事做出的反应要敏捷恰当。只要养成正确的思维和行动习惯，任何目标都可望达成。

◎ 要始终保持正确的态度——积极的心态。

BUILD A POSITIVE MENTAL ATTITUDE

◎ Create and maintain a positive mental attitude through your own willpower, based on motives of your own adaption.

◎ Be sensitive to your own reactions by controlling your emotional responses. Believe that any goal can be achieved. Develop right habits of thought and action.

◎ Maintain the right attitude-a positive mental attitude!

积极的心态是一种无法抗拒的力量，
没有任何一种事物能如它一般坚定不移。

拥有积极心态的人总是能找出可行之路，
而持消极心态的人却总是找出种种不可为之的理由。

改变你的心态，
你周围的世界也将为之而改变。

A positive mental attitude is an
irresistible force that knows no such
thing as an immovable object.

A positive mind finds a way it
can be done; a negative mind looks
for all the ways it can't be done.

Change your mental attitude
and the world around you
will change accordingly.

Lesson 8

Enthusiasm

Enthusiasm Inspires Action and is the Most Contagious of all Emotions

第 8 课
充满热情

热情足以激励行动，
它是所有情感中最富有感染力的。

Enthusiasm is faith in action. It is the intense emotion known as burning desire. It comes from within, although it radiates outwardly in the expression of one's voice and countenance.

Enthusiasm is power because it is the instrument by which adversities and failures and temporary defeats may be transmuted into action backed by faith. The flame of enthusiasm burning within you turns thought into action.

热情将信念转化为行动。它是一种强烈的情感，犹如燃烧的欲望。它发自于内心，尽管它以声音、面部表情等方式流露。

热情是一种力量，因为借助于它，任何逆境、失败以及暂时的挫折都可以转化为由信念支撑的行动。你内心熊熊燃烧的热情的火焰，是将思想转变为行动的基础。

保持你的热情

◎ 要对你期望的目标充满热情，日复一日地专注于这一目标。你的目标越值得拥有，越令你渴望，你就会对它越来越专心致志、热爱无比。

◎ 热情因为积极思维和积极行动而得以不断增长。掌控好热情的关键在于：始终如一地将热情集中于值得拥有的目标，一旦你把热情都用到某一目标上，它必将引领你勇往直前。

CONTROL YOUR ENTHUSIASM

◎ To become enthusiastic about achieving a desirable goal, keep your mind on that goal day after day. The more worthy and desirable your objectives, the more dedicated and enthusiastic you will become.

◎ Enthusiasm thrives on a positive mind and positive action. The key to controlling your enthusiasm: Always give it a worthy goal to focus on and once you have channeled it toward a goal, it will carry you forward.

热情推动想象的车轮转动。

Enthusiasm starts the wheels of imagination turning.

Lesson 9
Self-discipline

If You Direct Your Thoughts
and Control Your Emotions,
You Will Ordain Your Destiny.

第 9 课
高度的自制力

如果你能厘清自己的思路，
控制自己的情绪，
你就能决定自己的命运。

Self-discipline begins with the mastery of thought. If you do not control your thoughts, you cannot control your needs. Self-discipline calls for a balancing of the emotions of your heart with the reasoning faculty of your head.

Self-discipline is the bottleneck through which all of your personal power for success must flow. We have the power of self-determination, the ability to choose what our thoughts and actions will be.

高度的自制力始于对思维的掌控。如果你不能厘清自己的思路，你自然无法把控自身的需求。自制力往往需要兼顾理智与情感，平衡一个人内心的情感与其大脑的思考能力。

自制力可以说是一条管道，而一个人为了达到成功的目标所必须的所有力量，都会流经这个管道。我们每个人都有能力自我掌控，有能力选择个人的思维与行动。

加强自制力

◎自制力有助于一个人培养和保持良好的习惯，使其可以将其所有的注意力都锁定在他所渴望的目标上，并且一直保持这种状态直到目标达成。

◎如果一个人不能控制自己的思想，他同样无法控制自己的行动。三思而后行。通过自我约束力，一个人可以逐步形成自己的思维模式，与自己的目标相协调。

ENFORCE SELF-DISCIPLINE

◎ Self-discipline is perhaps the most important function in aiding an individual in the development and maintenance of habits. Self-discipline enables a person to fix his or her entire attention upon any desired purpose and hold it there until that purpose has been attained.

◎ If you do not control your thoughts, you do not control your deeds. Think first and act afterward. Self-discipline is the principle by which you may voluntarily shape the patterns of your thoughts to harmonize with your goals and purposes.

自制力，或是自我控制力，
意味着你要控制自己的思维。
要想控制别人，先要控制自己。
自制力是领导成功的首要准则。

Self-discipline, or self-control, means taking possession of your own mind.

Before trying to master others, be sure you are the master of yourself.

Self-discipline is the first rule of all successful leadership.

Lesson 10
Accurate Thinking
Truth Will be Truth,
Regardless of a Closed Mind, Ignorance,
or the Refusal to Believe.

第 10 课
缜密的思考

无论你因循守旧、愚钝无知或是拒绝相信，
真理永远是真理。

The power of thought is the most dangerous or the most beneficial power available, depending on how it is used.

Through the power of thought man builds great empires of civilization.

Accurate thinking is based on two major fundamentals:

◎ *inductive* reasoning, based on the assumption of unknown facts and hypotheses; and

◎ *deductive* reasoning, based on known facts or what are believed to be facts.

思考的力量究竟是我们所拥有的最危险的力量，还是最有用的力量，取决于我们如何运用它。人类正是通过思考的力量创建了伟大的文明帝国。

缜密的思考建立在两大重要的基本原则之上：

归纳推理，以对未知事实的设想和假说为根据，以及；

演绎推理，以已知事实或公认的事实为根据。

缜密思考

◎ 当你学会了如何鉴别、如何联系、如何吸收和应用某些准则来达到自己的目标时，你就可以从他人和自己的经历中学习和汲取经验。

◎ 学会把事实和虚构或是道听途说区分开来，学会将事实划分为重要和不重要两个类别。

◎ 慎重对待他人的观点。别人的观点也可能是危险的、毁灭性的。要确保你的观点并非他人的偏见。

THINK ACCURATELY

◎ Be careful of others' opinions. They could be dangerous and destructive. Make sure your opinions are not someone else' s prejudices.

◎ You can learn from your own experiences as well as those of others when you learn how to recognize, relate, assimilate, and apply principles in order to achieve your goals.

◎ Learn to separate facts from fiction or hearsay evidence. Learn to separate facts into classes-important and unimportant.

习惯缜密思考的人不会让任何人干扰他思考。

Accurate thinkers permit no one to do their thinking for them

Lesson 11
Controlled Thinking

Keep Your Mind on the Things You Want
And Off the Things You Don' t Want!

第 11 课 调控好思维方向

专注于你想要达到的目标，
而不去想那些你不想要的结果。

Controlled attention is organized mind power. Is is the highest form of self-discipline. It is the act of coordinating all the faculties of the mind and directing their combined power to a given end or definite objective.

Controlled attention leads to a mastery in any type of human endeavor because it enables one to focus the powers of his mind upon the attainment of a definite objective and to keep it so directed at will. Great achievements come from minds that are at peace with themselves.

Peace within one' s mind is not a matter of luck but is a priceless possession, which can be attained only by self-discipline based upon controlled attention.

控制注意力就是理性的思维力，它是自制力的最高形式。它可以协调你大脑所有的官能，将它们调动起来的力量运用于某一既定的或是明确的目标。

控制注意力可以掌控任何一种人类行为模式，因为它能把一个人大脑所有的能量集中在达成某一明确的目标上，且能有效管理这一目标。伟大的成功来源于内心的定力。

内心的定力无关乎运气，而是一笔宝贵的财富。这种定力唯有通过专注力基础之上的自律才能得以实现。

控制你的注意力

◎ 如果你主动地将注意力集中在特定目标的积极方面，并使之成为日常习惯，迫使自己对目标进行全神贯注的思考，那你就是在调动潜意识为实现这一目标而努力。

◎ 一个能控制自己思维的人必能控制其他一切事物。你的大脑就应该用于经常思考那些有助于达到你所渴望的目标的事情。

CONTROL YOUR ATTENTION

◎ When you voluntarily fix your attention upon a definite major purpose of a positive nature and force your mind through your daily habits of thought to dwell on the subject, you condition your subconscious mind to act on that purpose.

◎ The person who controls his or her own mind may control everything else. Keep your mind busy with thought material that may be helpful in attaining the object of your desire.

HONG KONG

控制你大脑的思考，

你就永不会受到他人思维的干扰。

财富源于思考。

积极的思考去解决问题远胜于祈祷，

难题能不攻自破。

Control your own mind and you may never be controlled by the mind of another.

Riches begin with thoughts.

Thinking your way through your Problems is safer than wishing your way through them.

Lesson 12
Teamwork

Teamwork Costs So Little in Time and Effort, And it Pays Huge Dividends.

第 12 课
团队合作

团队合作在时间和精力上花费甚少，
却回报丰厚。

Teamwork is harmonious cooperation that is willing, volutary, and free. Whenever the spirit of teamwork is the dominating influence in business or industry, success is inevitable.

Harmonious cooperation is a priceless asset that you can acquire in proportion to your giving.

Teamwork, in a spirit of friendliness, costs little in the way of time and effort. Generosity, fair treatment, courtesy, and a willingness to serve are qualities that pay high dividends whenever they are applied in human relations.

团队合作是一种自愿、自发、自由的协调互补合作。无论什么时候，只要团队精神在某一企业或某一行业中起着主导作用，成功就是必然的事情。

协调合作是无价的财富，它与你的付出是成比例的。

团队合作，其本质就是一种友好精神，在时间和精力方面花费甚少。慷慨大方，公正处事，礼貌待人，服务精神，人际关系中无论什么时候运用这些品质都会让你获益颇丰。

激励团队合作

◎ 团队合作创造力量。自愿合作的团队精神所产生的力量会一直持续下去，只要自愿的精神存在。

◎ 团队合作使个人和企业获得发展，并且为他们提供无限的机会。

◎ 与人分享，加倍增长；拒绝给予，日渐枯竭。

INSPIRE TEAMWORK

◎ Teamwork produces power. The power produced by teamwork made by willing cooperation will endure as long as that spirit of willingness prevails.

◎ Teamwork builds individuals and businesses and provides unlimited opportunity for all.

◎ That which you share will multiply; that which you withhold will diminish.

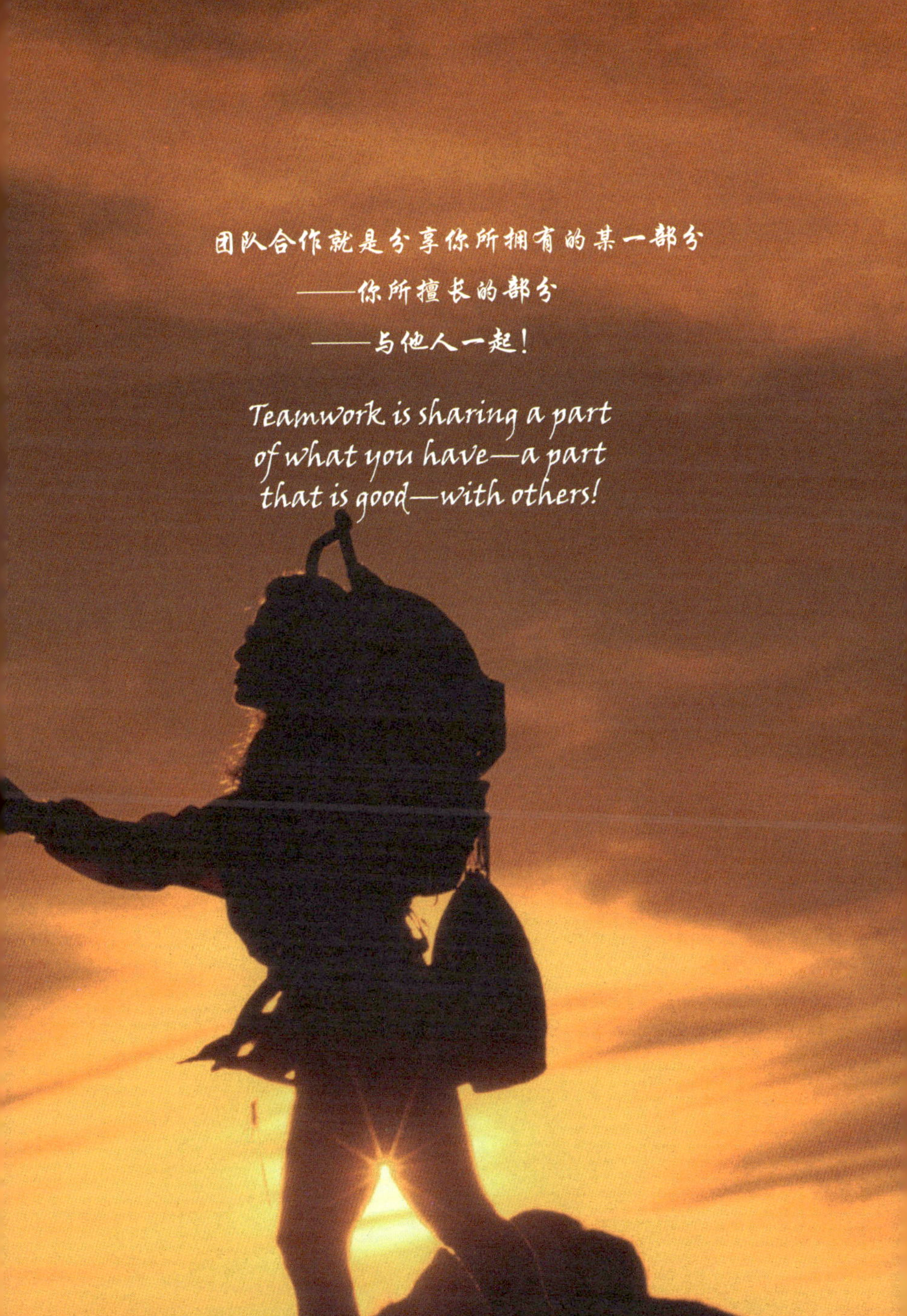
团队合作就是分享你所拥有的某一部分
——你所擅长的部分
——与他人一起！
Teamwork is sharing a part
of what you have—a part
that is good—with others!

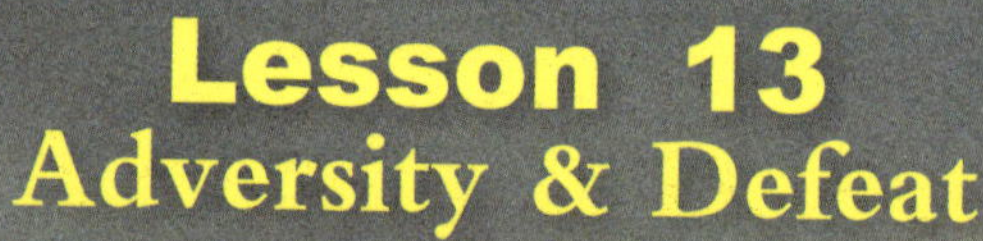

Lesson 13

Adversity & Defeat

Every Adversity You Meet Carries With it a Seed of Equivalent or Greater Benefit.

第 13 课
逆境与挫败

每一次遭遇逆境，
都会给你带来同等甚至更大的收益。

Defeat may be a stepping-stone or a stumbling block according to your mental attitude and how you relate to it yourself. It is never the same as failure unless and until it has been accepted as such.

Many so-called failures represent only a temporary defeat that may prove to be a blessing in disguise.

Your mental attitude in respect to defeat is the factor of major importance that determines whether you rise with the tides of fortune or misfortune.

挫折究竟是垫脚石还是绊脚石，完全取决于你的心态和你如何理解它。它从来都不等同于失败，除非你自己这样认为，也只有当你这样对待它时，挫折才会真正变成失败。

许多所谓的失败其实只不过是暂时的挫折，事后往往会证明因祸得福。

你对挫折的心态是决定你将交好运还是交厄运的重要因素。

从逆境和挫折中学习

◎ 个人的成功往往和个人的经历及战胜过的挫折成正比。

◎ 记住：你所碰到的最糟糕的事情，也许会是你所能遇到的最美好的事情的前站，只要不让它把你最美好的东西夺走。

LEARN FROM ADVERSITY AND DEFEAT

◎ Individal success usually is in exact proportion to the scope of the defeat the individual has experienced and mastered.

◎ Remember: The worst that can happen to you may be the best thing that can happen to you if you don't let it get the best of you.

5683

学会让逆境之风扬起你的人生之帆。

不要沉溺于失败中。

如果你将挫折看作是一种激励，激励你带着全新的信心与决心再次尝试，那么获得成功只是时间的问题。

Learn to use the winds of
adversity to sail your ship of life.

Close the door of your
mind on all failure.

If you accept defeat as an inspiration
to try again with renewed confidence
and determination, attaining success
will only be a matter of time.

Lesson 14
Creative Vision
Only an Open Mind Can Grow.

第 14 课
创新致胜

只有开放性的思维才会让你不断发展。

Our greatest gift is our thinking mind. It analyzes, compares, It creates, visualizes, foresees, and generates ideas.

Imagination is your mind's exercise, challenge,and adventure. It is the key to all of a person's achievements, the mainspring of all human endeavor, the secret door to the soul of a person.

Creative vision may be an inborn quality of mind, or an acquired quality, for it may be developed by the the free and fearless use of the faculty of imagination.

我们人类最大的天赋就是有会思考的大脑。它会分析、比较、选择，它能创造、想象、预见、形成观点。

想象就是你的大脑在进行练习、挑战和冒险。它是一个人取得所有成就的关键，是整个人类努力的主要推动力，是通往一个人灵魂的秘密之门。

创新致胜也许是大脑与生俱来的一种属性，也可能是后天习得的一种品质，因为它可以通过自由无畏地运用想象力从而获得自身的发展。

要有创造性思维

◎ 让自己才思泉涌的方式之一是留出时间，培养学习、思考和规划的习惯。

◎ 保持安静、平和，倾听你内心深处坚毅的呼唤，冥想那些助你达成目标的方法。

CULTIVATE CREATIVE VISION

◎ One of the ways to increase your flow of ideas is by developing the habit of taking study time, thinking time, and planning time.

◎ Be quiet and motionless, and listen for that small, still voice that speaks from within you. Contemplate the ways in which you can achieve your objectives.

想象力就像是一个灵魂工厂，
其中所有的计划都是为了个人成就而制定的。
Imagination is the workshop of the
soul wherein all plans are shaped
for individual achievement.

Lesson 15
Health

A Sound Physical Health is Dependent
Upon a Positive Mental Attitude.

第 15 课
保持身心健康

强健的体魄依赖于积极的心态。

You are a mind with a body. Inasmuch as your brain controls your body, recognize that sound physical health demands a positive mental attitude, a health consciousness.

To maintain a health consciousness, one must think in terms of sound health, not in terms of illness and disease. Remember, what your mind focuses upon, your mind brings into existence.

每个人都是身心合一的。因为你的大脑控制你的身体，你必须意识到强健的体魄须有积极的心态，健康的心态。

要保持健康的心态，你必须从内心对健康活力充满希望，而不是时时对身体状况忧心忡忡。记住，你的思维集中在哪种状态，你思考的结果也渐渐随之成形。

◎ 要对发展和保持健康心态持一种积极的状态，就要运用自制力，让大脑远离消极的想法和消极的影响，创造和保持一种稳定的生活状态。

◎ 劳逸结合，有张有弛，身心努力，严肃中带有幽默，这样你就踏上了健康与幸福的大道。

◎ 饮食得当，积极思考，适量睡眠再加上适当的娱乐，你就可以把看医生的钱省下来用作度假。

MAINTAIN SOUND HEALTH

◎ To maintain a positive attitude for the development and maintenance of a sound health consciousness, use self-discipline, keep your mind free of negative thoughts and influence, and create and maintain a well-balanced life.

◎ Follow work with play, mental effort with physical effort, and seriousness with humor, and you will be on the road to good health and happiness.

影响身体的任何事情最终也会影响你的思维；

反之亦然。

不要想着如何治愈头疼，

更恰当的办法应该是找到引起头疼的原因并解决它。

Eat right, think right, sleep right, and play right and you can save the doctor's bill for your vacation.

Whatever affects the body will affect the mind; whatever affects the mind will affect the body.

Don't try to cure a headache. It's better to cure the thing that caused it.

Lesson 16
Budgeting Time & Money

The Successful Person Budgets Time,
Income and Expenditures,
Living Within His Means.

第 16 课
合理安排时间和金钱

成功人士会合理安排时间、收入和支出，
做到量入为出。

Time and money are precious resources, and few people striving for success ever believe they possess either one in excess.Understanding how you use them is an important part of evaluating your progress toward success and analyzing what may be holding you back.

Learn to budget your time to the important tasks and your money to those things related to your definite purpose.

时间和金钱是宝贵的资源。为成功而奋斗的人们总会觉得自己时间或金钱不够用。了解自己该如何使用时间和金钱是很重要的，这有助于你评估成功的进展，分析阻挠你成功的因素。

学会规划时间，把它花在重要的任务上；学会预算支出，把钱花在与你既定目标有关的事情上。

合理安排你的时间和金钱

◎ 不论是个人还是企业，都需要巧妙而平衡地使用时间和金钱。把自己和自己做过的事情列个清单，就很清楚自己把时间和金钱花在了哪里，怎么花的。

◎ 不要浪费时间或者金钱。你可以将自己收入的十分之一存起来或者用于投资。就像任何优秀企业一样，把钱做好预算，合理地使用时间，朝着你的目标前进。

BUDGET YOUR TIME AND MONEY

◎ Intelligently balance your use of time and resources, both business and personal. Take inventory of yourself and your activities so that you discover where and how you are spending your time and your money.

◎ Don't waste your time or your money. Ten percent of all you earn is yours to keep and invest. Like any good business, budget your money, and use your time wisely toward the attainment of your objectives.

SW
W
NW
N
125·65
263·56
325·68
156·85

不少人的失败在于漠视时间和金钱的重要，
轻视时光，任意挥霍它们。

*Failures squander time and
income with conternptuous
disregard for their value.*

Lesson 17
Habits

You are Where You are and What You are Because of Your Established Habits, Thoughts, And Deeds.

第 17 课
养成良好的习惯

正因为你既定的习惯、想法和行为，
你才是今天的状态，成为了现在的你。

All of us are ruled by habits. They are fastened upon us by repeated thoughts and experiences. We create patterns of thought by repeating certain ideas or behavior and making them permanent.

Some habits are good and some are bad. Many we are aware of, but some we are blinded to. Each habit begins is the mind, consciously or subconsciously. Each can be developed and neutralized or changed at will through the proper use of your mind.

我们每一个人都受到习惯的控制。习惯通过重复的想法与经历和我们紧紧联系在一起。我们不断重复某些观点或行为并使之永久化，从而形成自己的思维模式。

有好习惯，也有坏习惯。有些习惯我们意识到了，有些我们视而不见。每一种习惯都始于头脑的意识，无论你是有意识的或是下意识的。我们可以适度利用思维来刻意地培养、中止或者改变每一种习惯。

养成良好的习惯

◎ 要养成一种习惯才可以替代另一种习惯。

◎ 培养积极的习惯，与达到你的目标相协调。

◎ 播种一个行为，收获一种习惯；

◎ 播种一种习惯，收获一类性格；

◎ 播种一类性格，收获一个命运。

CREATE GOOD HABRRS

◎ It takes a habit to replace a habit.

◎ Develop positive habits that will be in harmony with the achievement of your definite purpose or goal.

◎ Sow an act, reap a habit.
◎ Sow a habit, reap a character.
◎ Sow a character, reap a destiny.

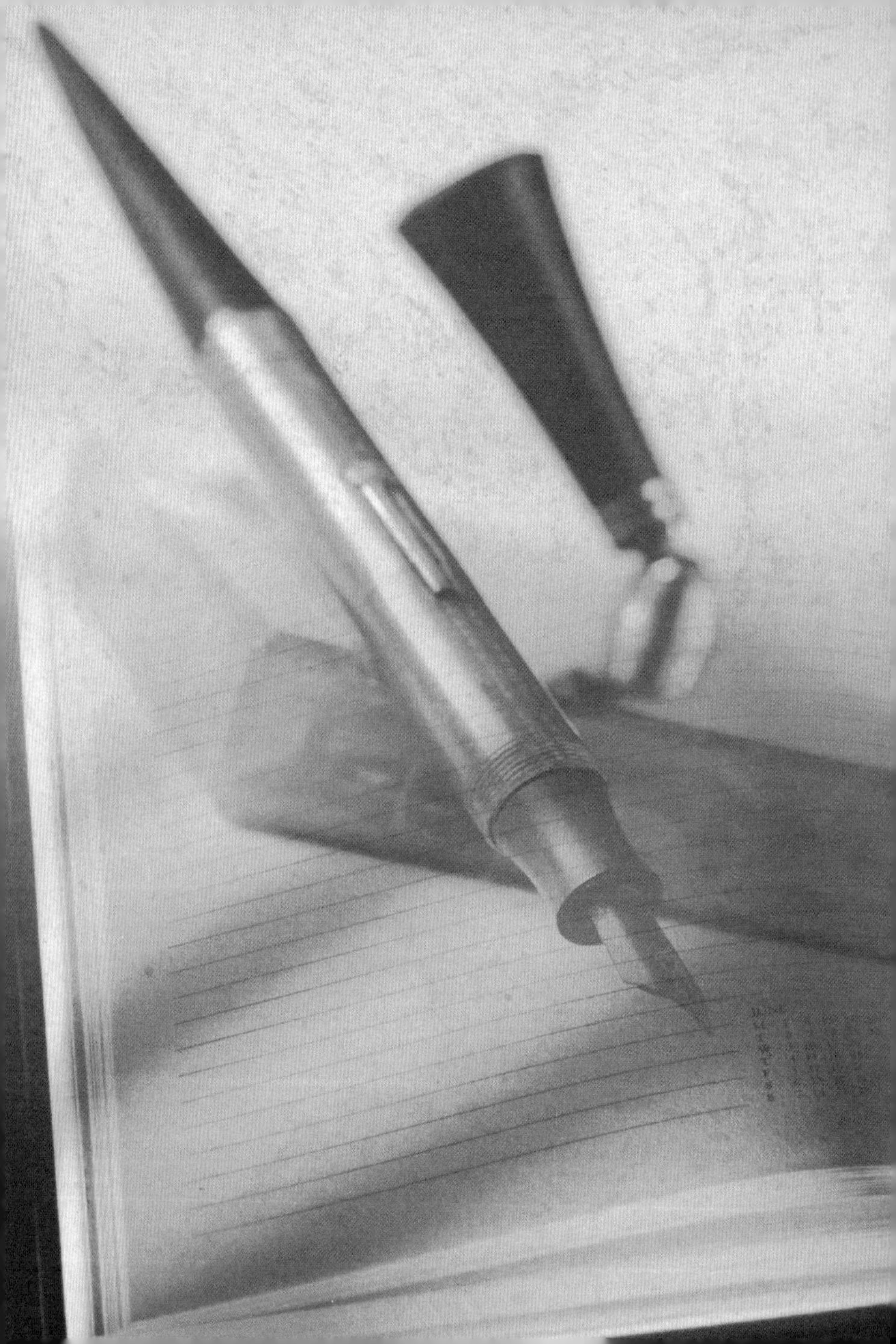

一个坏习惯可能会毁掉许多好习惯。

我们可以形成自己的习惯，

只有人类被赐予了这种特质和手段。

你会受到习惯的控制——无论是好习惯还是坏习惯！

One bad habit often spoils
a dozen good ones.

Only man has been given
the privilege and the means
to fix his own habits.

You are ruled by your habits—
good or bad!

ABOUT NAPOLEON HILL

Napoleon Hill was a pioneer in the study of the American philosophy of personal achievement and is considered the founder of the modern genre of personal-success literature. The success formulas he developed through his research have helped millions of people throughout the world achieve outstanding results in every aspect of life.

Hill was born october 26, 1883,in a two-room log cabin in the mountains of Wise County, Virginia, a region marked by illiteracy and grinding poverty. An unruly child who idolized Jesse James, his life was transformed by his stepmother's suggestion that he put his keen imagination and initiative to use as a writer. At age 15, he completed grade school and began to work part time as a "mountain reporter" for local, small-town newspapers, then as a reporter for *Bob Taylor' s Magazine,* interviewing and writing "success profiles" of famous individuals.

In 1908, while on assignment, Hill met Pittsburgh

关于拿破仑·希尔

拿破仑·希尔是美国成功学研究方面的先驱，他被认为是现代成功学的奠基者。他通过研究得出的成功信条已经帮助全世界成千上万的人们在生活的各个领域取得了杰出的成就。

希尔于1883年10月26日出生于弗吉尼亚州阿巴拉契亚山怀斯县的偏远山区，家境贫寒，家里只有两间小木屋。这一地区多年缺乏教育，贫困不堪。儿童时代的希尔不服管教，非常崇拜杰西·詹姆士（Jesse James），他的人生之所以后来能够改变，完全是得益于他继母的建议和支持。他把自己丰富的想象力和主动性都用在从事写作方面。15岁时，他完成了小学学业，开始在一家本地的小镇报纸兼职担任“mountain reporter”专栏作家，之后他又成为《鲍勃·泰勒杂志》（Bob Taylor's Magazine）的记者，采访名人，撰写他们的“成功传略”。

1908年，希尔在进行采访任务时，遇到了匹兹堡的工业家、当时世界上最富有的人——安德鲁·卡耐基。此次会面之后，将近20年里希尔进行的研究都得到了卡耐基的建议和非正式的资助——这直接促成了《成功学法则》的出版，希尔在本书中分享了他在研究过程中搜集来的观点和人生哲学。

本书出版后大受好评，为他奠定了成功学先驱的地位。1937年，他的另一著作《思考致富》为读者提供了个人成功学

industrialist Andrew Carnegie, then the richest man in the world. That meeting—and almost 20 years of subsequent research by Hill that was suggested and informally sponsored by Carnegie—led to the publication of *Law of success*, which shared the ideas and philosophy gleaned from his research. The book won wide acclaim and established Hill as a leader in the success movement. In 1937, *Think and Grow Rich!* Provided readers with the steps for forming a philosophy of personal achievement.

Hill' s popularity led to him becoming an informal advisor to two U.S. presidents—Woodrow Wilson and Franklin D. Roosevelt. He would go on to author more than 30 books, including *Success through a Positive Mental Attitude*, written with W.Clement Stone. Hill was a fixture on the motivational lecture and a prolific creator of textbooks, study guides, and other success materials.

During his career, Hill founded three magazines—*Hill' s Golden Rule in 1919, Napoleon Hill' s Magazine* in 1921, and *Inspiration Magazine* in 1931. An ardent admirer of Orison Swett Marden, he revived *SUCCESS* magazine and served as its editor. In 1954, he joined with Stone to found *Success Unlimited* magazine.

Hill died on November 8, 1970, at his retirement home on Paris Mountain Near Greenville, South Carolina, where he spent the last 18 years of his life.

形成的基础。

希尔的大受欢迎使得他成为两任美国总统——伍德罗·威尔逊总统和富兰克林·D·罗斯福总统的非正式顾问。他又继续撰写了30多本书，包括与W·克莱门特·斯通（W. Clement Stone）合著的《积极思考带来成功》。希尔经常作一些启发性的巡回讲座，他还是一名多产的创作家，作品包括课本、学习指南以及其他一些成功学方面的内容。

希尔在他的职业生涯中创办了三本杂志——1919年的《希尔的黄金法则》，1921年的《拿破仑·希尔》杂志，以及1931年的《灵感杂志》。希尔极度崇拜奥里森·S·马登（Orison Swett Marden），他使《成功》杂志复刊，并成为该杂志的编辑。1954年，他与斯通一起创办了《成功无限》杂志。

希尔退休后居住在南卡罗莱纳州格林维尔城附近的帕里斯山的一家养老院，他在那里度过了生命中最后的18年，于1970年11月8日逝世。